Book 1
Android Programming In a Day!
BY SAM KEY

&

Book 2
HTML Professional Programming Made Easy
BY SAM KEY

Book 1
Android Programming In a Day!

BY SAM KEY

The Power Guide for Beginners In Android App Programming

Programming Box Set #80: Android Programming in a Day & HTML Professional Programming Made Easy

Copyright 2015 by Sam Key - All rights reserved.

Table Of Contents

Introduction

I want to thank you and congratulate you for purchasing the book, "Introduction to Android Programming in a Day – The Power Guide for Beginners in Android App Programming".

This book contains proven steps and strategies on how to get started with Android app development.

This book will focus on preparing you with the fun and tiring world of Android app development. Take note that this book will not teach you on how to program. It will revolve around the familiarization of the Android SDK and Eclipse IDE.

Why not focus on programming immediately? Unfortunately, the biggest reason many aspiring Android developers stop on learning this craft is due to the lack of wisdom on the Android SDK and Eclipse IDE.

Sure, you can also make apps using other languages like Python and other IDEs on the market. However, you can expect that it is much more difficult than learning Android's SDK and Eclipse's IDE.

On the other hand, you can use tools online to develop your Android app for you. But where's the fun in that? You will not learn if you use such tools. Although it does not mean that you should completely stay away from that option.

Anyway, the book will be split into four chapters. The first will prepare you and tell you the things you need before you develop apps. The second will tell you how you can configure your project. The third will introduce you to the Eclipse IDE. And the last chapter will teach you on how to run your program in your Android device.

Also, this book will be sprinkled with tidbits about the basic concepts of Android app development. And as you read along, you will have an idea on what to do next.

Thanks again for purchasing this book, I hope you enjoy it!

Chapter 1: Preparation

Android application development is not easy. You must have some decent background in program development. It is a plus if you know Visual Basic and Java. And it will be definitely a great advantage if you are familiar or have already used Eclipse's IDE (Integrated Development Environment). Also, being familiar with XML will help you.

You will need a couple of things before you can start developing apps.

First, you will need a high-end computer. It is common that other programming development kits do not need a powerful computer in order to create applications. However, creating programs for Android is a bit different. You will need more computing power for you to run Android emulators, which are programs that can allow you to test your programs in your computer.

Using a weak computer without a decent processor and a good amount of RAM will only make it difficult for you to run those emulators. If you were able to run it, it will run slowly.

Second, you will need an Android device. That device will be your beta tester. With it, you will know how your program will behave in an Android device. When choosing the test device, make sure that it is at par with the devices of the market you are targeting for your app. If you are targeting tablet users, use a tablet. If you are targeting smartphones, then use a smartphone.

Third, you will need the Android SDK (Software Development Kit) from Google. The SDK is a set of files and programs that can allow you to create and compile your program's code. As of this writing, the latest Android SDK's file size is around 350mb. It will take you 15 – 30 minutes to download it. If you uncompressed the Android SDK file, it will take up around 450mb of your computer's disk space. The link to the download page is: http://developer.android.com/sdk/index.html

The SDK can run on Windows XP, Windows 7, Mac OSX 10.8.5 (or higher), and Linux distros that can run 32bit applications and has glibc (GNU C library) 2.11 or higher.

Once you have unpacked the contents of the file you downloaded, open the SDK Manager. That program is the development kit's update tool. To make sure you have the latest versions of the kit's components, run the manager once in a while and download those updates. Also, you can use the SDK Manager to download older versions of SDK. You must do that in case you want to make programs with devices with dated Android operating systems.

Chapter 2: Starting Your First Project

To start creating programs, you will need to open Eclipse. The Eclipse application file can be found under the eclipse folder on the extracted files from the Android SDK. Whenever you run Eclipse, it will ask you where you want your Eclipse workspace will be stored. You can just use the default location and just toggle the don't show checkbox.

New Project

To start a new Android application project, just click on the dropdown button of the New button on Eclipse's toolbar. A context menu will appear, and click on the Android application project.

The New Android Application project details window will appear. In there, you will need to input some information for your project. You must provide your program's application name, project name, and package name. Also, you can configure the minimum and target SDK where your program can run and the SDK that will be used to compile your code. And lastly, you can indicate the default theme that your program will use.

Application Name

The application name will be the name that will be displayed on the Google's Play Store when you post it there. The project name will be more of a file name for Eclipse. It will be the project's identifier. It should be unique for every project that you build in Eclipse. By default, Eclipse will generate a project and package name for your project when you type something in the Application Name text box.

Package Name

The package name is not usually displayed for users. Take note that in case you will develop a large program, you must remember that your package name should never be changed. On the other hand, it is common that package names are the reverse of your domain name plus your project's name. For example, if your website's domain name is www.mywebsite.com and your project's name is Hello World, a good package name for your project will be com.mywebsite.helloworld.

The package name should follow the Java package name convention. The naming convention is there to prevent users from having similar names, which could result to numerous conflicts. Some of the rules you need to follow for the package name are:

• Your package name should be all in lower caps. Though Eclipse will accept a package name with a capital letter, but it is still best to adhere to standard practice.

• The reverse domain naming convention is included as a standard practice.

• Avoid using special characters in the package name. Instead, you can replace it with underscores.

• Also, you should never use or include the default com.example in your package name. Google Play will not accept an app with a package name like that.

Minimum SDK

Minimum required SDK could be set to lower or the lowest version of Android. Anything between the latest and the set minimum required version can run your program. Setting it to the lowest, which is API 1 or Android 1.0, can make your target audience wider.

Setting it to Android 2.2 (Froyo) or API 8, can make your program run on almost 95% of all Android devices in the world. The drawback fn this is that the features you can include in your program will be limited. Adding new features will force your minimum required SDK to move higher since some of the new functions in Android is not available on lower versions of the API (Application Programming Interface).

Target SDK

The target SDK should be set to the version of Android that most of your target audience uses. It indicates that you have tested your program to that version. And it means that your program is fully functional if they use it on a device that runs the target Android version.

Whenever a new version of Android appears, you should also update the target SDK of your program. Of course, before you release it to the market again, make sure that you test it on an updated device.

If a device with the same version as your set target SDK runs your program, it will not do any compatibility behavior or adjust itself to run the program. By default, you should set it to the highest version to attract your potential app buyers. Setting a lower version for your target SDK would make your program old and dated. By the way, the target SDK should be always higher or equal with the minimum target SDK version.

Compile with

The compile with version should be set to the latest version of Android. This is to make sure that your program will run on almost all versions down to the minimum version you have indicated, and to take advantage of the newest features and optimization offered by the latest version of Android. By default, the Android SDK will only have one version available for this option, which is API 20 or Android 4.4 (KitKat Wear).

After setting those all up, it is time to click on the Next button. The new page in the screen will contain some options such as creating custom launcher icon and creating activity. As of now, you do not need to worry about those. Just leave the default values and check, and click the Next button once again.

Custom Launcher Icon

Since you have left the Create Custom Launcher option checked, the next page will bring you in the launcher icon customization page. In there, you will be given three options on how you would create your launcher. Those options are launcher icons made from an image, clipart, or text.

With the text and clipart method, you can easily create an icon you want without thinking about the size and quality of the launcher icon. With those two, you can just get a preset image from the SDK or Android to use as a launcher icon. The same goes with the text method since all you need is to type the letters you want to appear on the icon and the SDK will generate an icon based on that.

The launcher icon editor also allows you to change the background and foreground color of your icon. Also, you can scale the text and clipart by changing the value of the additional padding of the icon. And finally, you can add simple 3D shapes on your icon to make it appear more professional.

Bitmap Iconography Tips

When it comes to images, you need to take note of a few reminders. First, always make sure that you will use vector images. Unlike the typical bitmap images (pictures taken from cameras or images created using Paint), vector images provide accurate and sharp images. You can scale it multiple times, but its sharpness will not disappear and will not pixelate. After all, vector images do not contain information about pixels. It only has numbers and location of the colors and lines that will appear in it. When it is scaled, it does not perform antialiasing or stretching since its image will be mathematically rendered.

In case that you will be the one creating or designing the image that you will use for your program and you will be creating a bitmap image, make sure that you start with a large image. A large image is easier to create and design.

Also, since in Android, multiple sizes of your icon will be needed, a large icon can make it easier for you to make smaller ones. Take note that if you scale a big picture into a small one, some details will be lost, but it will be easier to edit and fix and it will still look crisp. On the other hand, if you scale a small image into a big one, it will pixelate and insert details that you do not intend to show such as jagged and blurred edges.

Nevertheless, even when scaling down a big image into a smaller one, do not forget to rework the image. Remember that a poor-looking icon makes people think that the app you are selling is low-quality. And again, if you do not want to go through all that, create a vector image instead.

Also, when you create an image, make sure that it will be visible in any background. Aside from that, it is advisable to make it appear uniform with other Android icons. To do that, make sure that your image has a distinct silhouette that will make it look like a 3D image. The icon should appear as if you were looking above it and as if the source of light is on top of the image. The topmost part of the icon should appear lighter and the bottom part should appear darker.

Activity

Once you are done with your icon, click on the Next button. The page will now show the Activity window. It will provide you with activity templates to work on. The window has a preview box where you can see what your app will look like for every activity template. Below the selection, there is a description box that will tell you what each template does. For now, select the Blank Activity and click Next. The next page will ask you some details regarding the activity. Leave it on its default values and click Finish.

Once you do that, Eclipse will setup your new project. It might take a lot of time, especially if you are using a dated computer. The next chapter will discuss the programming interface of Eclipse.

Chapter 3: Getting Familiar with Eclipse and Contents of an Android App

When Eclipse has finished its preparation, you will be able to start doing something to your program. But hold onto your horses; explore Eclipse first before you start fiddling with anything.

Editing Area

In the middle of the screen, you will see a preview of your program. In it, you will see your program's icon beside the title of your program. Just left of it is the palette window. It contains all the elements that you can place in your program.

Both of these windows are inside Eclipse's editing area. You will be spending most of your time here, especially if you are going to edit or view something in your code or layout.

The form widgets tab will be expanded in the palette by default. There you will see the regular things you see in an Android app such as buttons, radio buttons, progress bar (the circle icon that spins when something is loading in your device or the bar the fills up when your device is loading), seek bar, and the ratings bar (the stars you see in reviews).

Aside from the form widgets, there are other elements that you can check and use. Press the horizontal tabs or buttons and examine all the elements you can possibly use in your program.

To insert a widget in your program, you can just drag the element you want to include from the palette and drop it in your program's preview. Eclipse will provide you visual markers and grid snaps for you to place the widgets you want on the exact place you want. Easy, right?

Take note, some of the widgets on the palette may require higher-level APIs or versions of Android. For example, the Grid Layout from the Layouts section of the palette requires API 14 (Android 4.0 Ice Cream Sandwich) or higher. If you add it in your program, it will ask you if you want to install it. In case you did include and install it, remember that it will not be compatible for older versions or any device running on API 13 and lower. It is advisable that you do not include any element that asks for installation. It might result into errors.

Output Area, Status Bar, and Problem Browser

On the bottom part of Eclipse, the status bar, problem browser, and output area can be found. It will contain messages regarding to the state of your project. If Eclipse found errors in your program, it will be listed there. Always check the Problems bar for any issues. Take note that you cannot run or compile your program if Eclipse finds at least one error on your project.

Navigation Pane

On the leftmost part of your screen is the navigation pane that contains the package explorer. The package explorer lets you browse all the files that are included in your project. Three of the most important files that you should know where to look for are:

•   activity_main.xml: This file is your program's main page or window. And it will be the initial file that will be opened when you create a new project. In case you accidentally close it on your editor window, you can find it at: YourProjectName > res > layout > activity_main.xml.

• MainActivity.java: As of now, you will not need to touch this file. However, it is important to know where it is since later in your Android development activities, you will need to understand it and its contents. It is located at: YourProjectName > src > YourPackageName > MainActivity.java.

• AndroidManifest.xml: It contains the essential information that you have set up a while ago when you were creating your project file in Eclipse. You can edit the minimum and target SDK in there. It is located at YourProjectName > AndroidManifest.xml.

Aside from those files, you should take note of the following directories:

• src/: This is where most of your program's source files will be placed. And your main activity file is locafile is located.

• res/: Most of the resources will be placed here. The resources are placed inside the subdirectories under this folder.

• res/drawable-hdpi/: Your high density bitmap files that you might show in your app will go in here.

• res/layout/: All the pages or interface in your app will be located here – including your activity_main.xml.

• res/values/: The values you will store and use in your program will be placed in this directory in form of XML files.

In the event that you will create multiple projects, remember that the directory for those other projects aside from the one you have opened will still be available in your package explorer. Because of that, you might get confused over the files you are working on. Thankfully, Eclipse's title bar indicates the location and name of the file you are editing, which makes it easier to know what is currently active on the editing area.

Outline Box

Displays the current structure of the file you are editing. The outline panel will help you visualize the flow and design of your app. Also, it can help you find the widgets you want to edit.

Properties Box

Whenever you are editing a layout file, the properties box will appear below the outline box. With the properties box, you can edit certain characteristics of a widget. For example, if you click on the Hello World text on the preview of your main activity layout file, the contents of the properties box will be populated. In there, you can edit the properties of the text element that you have clicked. You can change the text, height, width, and even its font color.

Menu and Toolbar

The menu bar contains all the major functionalities of Eclipse. In case you do not know where the button of a certain tool is located, you can just invoke that tool's function on the menu bar. On the other hand, the tool bar houses all the major functions in Eclipse. The most notable buttons there are the New, Save, and Run.

As of now, look around Eclipse's interface. Also, do not do or change anything on the main activity file or any other file. The next chapter will discuss about how to run your program. As of now, the initial contents of your project are also valid as an android program. Do not

change anything since you might produce an unexpected error.
Nevertheless, if you really do want to change something, go ahead.
You can just create another project for you to keep up with the next
chapter.

Chapter 4: Running Your Program

By this time, even if you have not done anything yet to your program, you can already run and test it in your Android device or emulator. Why teach this first before the actual programming? Well, unlike typical computer program development, Android app development is a bit bothersome when it comes to testing.

First, the program that you are developing is intended for Android devices. You cannot actually run it normally in your computer without the help of an emulator. And you will actually do a lot of testing. Even with the first lines of code or changes in your program, you will surely want to test it.

Second, the Android emulator works slow. Even with good computers, the emulator that comes with the Android SDK is painstakingly sluggish. Alternatively, you can use BlueStacks. BlueStacks is a free Android emulator that works better than the SDK's emulator. It can even run games with it! However, it is buggy and does not work well (and does not even run sometimes) with every computer.

This chapter will focus on running your program into your Android device. You will need to have a USB data cable and connect your computer and Android. Also, you will need to have the right drivers for your device to work as a testing platform for the programs you will develop. Unfortunately, this is the preferred method for most beginners since running your app on Android emulators can bring a lot more trouble since it is super slow. And that might even discourage you to continue Android app development.

Why Android Emulators are Slow

Why are Android emulators slow? Computers can run virtual OSs without any problems, but why cannot the Android emulator work fine? Running virtual OSs is not something as resource-extensive anymore with today's computer standards. However, with Android, you will actually emulate an OS together with a mobile device. And nowadays, these mobile devices are as powerful as some of the dated computers back then. Regular computers will definitely have a hard time with that kind of payload from an Android emulator.

USB Debugging Mode

To run your program in an Android device, connect your Android to your computer. After that, set your Android into USB debugging mode. Depending on the version of the Android device you are using, the steps might change.

For 3.2 and older Android devices:

Go to Settings > Applications > Development

For 4.0 and newer Android devices:

Go to Settings > Developer Options

For 4.2 and newer Android devices with hidden Developer Options:

Go to Settings > About Phone. After that, tap the Build Number seven times. Go back to the previous screen. The Developer Options should be visible now.

Android Device Drivers

When USB debugging is enabled, your computer will install the right drivers for the Android device that you have. If your computer does not have the right drivers, you will not be able to run your program on your device. If that happens to you, visit this page: http://developer.android.com/tools/extras/oem-usb.html. It contains instructions on how you can install the right driver for your device and operating system.

Running an App in Your Android Device Using Eclipse

Once your device is already connected and you have the right drivers for it, you can now do a test run of your application. On your Eclipse window, click the Run button on the toolbar or in the menu bar.

If a Run As window appeared, select the Android Application option and click on the OK button. After that, a dialog box will appear. It will provide you with two options: running the program on an Android device or on an AVD (Android Virtual Device) or emulator.

If your device was properly identified by your computer, it will appear on the list. Click on your device's name and click OK. Eclipse will compile your Android app, install it on your device, and then run it. That is how simple it is.

Take note, there will be times that your device will appear offline on the list. In case that happens, there are two simple fixes that you can do to make it appear online again: restart your device or disable and enable the USB debugging function on your device.

Now, you can start placing widgets on your main activity file. However, always make sure that you do not place any widgets that require higher APIs.

Conclusion

Thank you again for purchasing this book!

I hope this book was able to help you get started with Android Programming in a Day!.

The next step is to study the following:

View and Viewgroups: View and Viewgroups are the two types of objects that you will be dealing with Android. View objects are the elements or widgets that you see in Android programs. Viewgroup objects act as containers to those View objects.

Relative, Linear, and Table Layout: When it comes to designing your app, you need to know the different types of layouts. In later versions of Android, you can use other versions of layouts, but of course, the API requirements will go up if you use them. Master these, and you will be able to design faster and cleaner.

Adding Activities or Interface: Of course, you would not want your program to contain one page only. You need more. You must let your app customers to see more content and functions. In order to do that, you will need to learn adding activities to your program. This is the part when developing your Android app will be tricky. You will not be able to rely completely on the drag and drop function and graphical layout view of Eclipse. You will need to start typing some code into your program.

Adding the Action Bar: The action bar is one of the most useful elements in Android apps. It provides the best location for the most used functions in your program. And it also aid your users when switching views, tabs, or drop down list.

Once you have gain knowledge on those things, you will be able to launch a decent app on the market. The last thing you might want to do is to learn how to make your program support other Android devices.

You must know very well that Android devices come in all shapes and form. An Android device can be a tablet, a smartphone, or even a television. Also, they come with different screen sizes. You cannot just expect that all your customers will be using a 4-inch display smartphone. Also, you should think about the versions of Android they are using. Lastly, you must also add language options to your programs. Even though English is fine, some users will appreciate if your program caters to the primary language that they use.

And that is about it for this book. Make sure you do not stop learning Android app development.

Finally, if you enjoyed this book, please take the time to share your thoughts and post a review on Amazon. We do our best to reach out to readers and provide the best value we can. Your positive review will help us achieve that. It'd be greatly appreciated!

Thank you and good luck!

Book 2
HTML Professional
Programming Made Easy

BY SAM KEY

Expert HTML Programming
Language Success in a Day for any
Computer Users

Table Of Contents

Introduction

I want to thank you and congratulate you for purchasing the book, *Professional HTML Programming Made Easy: Expert HTML Programming Language Success In A Day for any Computer User!*

This book contains proven steps and strategies on how to create a web page in just a day. And if you have a lot of time in a day, you will be able to create a decent and informative website in two or three days.

HTML programming or development lessons are sometimes used as an introductory resource to programming and is a prerequisite to learning web development. In this book, you will be taught of the fundamentals of HTML. Mastering the contents of this book will make web development easier for you and will allow you to grasp some of the basics of computer programming.

To get ready for this book, you will need a desktop or laptop. That is all. You do not need to buy any expensive HTML or website development programs. And you do not need to rent a server or subscribe to a web hosting service. If you have questions about those statements, the answers are in the book.

Thanks again for purchasing this book. I hope you enjoy it!

Chapter 1: Getting Started with HTML

This book will assume that you have no prior knowledge on HTML. Do not skip reading any chapters or this book if you plan to learn about CSS, JavaScript, or any other languages that is related to web development.

HTML is a markup language. HTML defines what will be displayed on your browser and how it will be displayed. To program or code HTML, all you need is a text editor. If your computer is running on a Windows operating system, you can use Notepad to create or edit HTML files. Alternatively, if your computer is a Mac, you can use TextEdit instead.

Why is this book telling you to use basic text editors? Why are expert web developers using HTML creation programs such as Adobe Dreamweaver to create their pages? Those programs are supposed to make HTML coding easier, right?

You do not need them yet. Using one will only confuse you, especially if you do not know the fundamentals of HTML. Aside from that, web designing programs such as Adobe Dreamweaver are not all about dragging and dropping items on a web page. You will also need to be capable of manually writing the HTML code that you want on your page. That is why those programs have different views like Design and Code views. And most of them time, advanced developers stay and work more using the Code view, which is similar to a typical text editing program.

During your time learning HTML using this book, create a folder named HTML on your desktop. As you progress, you will see snippets of HTML code written here. You can try them out using your text editor and browser. You can save them as HTML files, place them into the HTML folder, and open them on your browser to see what those snippets of codes will do.

Your First HTML Page

Open your text editor and type the following in it:

Hello World!

After writing that line on your text editor, save it. On the save file dialog box, change the name of the file as firstexample.html. Do not forget the .html part. That part will serve as your file's file extension. It denotes that the file that you have saved is an HTML file and can be opened by the web browsers you have in your computer. Make sure that your program was able to save it as an .html file. Some text editor programs might still automatically add another file extension on your file name, so if that happens, you will not be open that file in your browser normally.

By the way, you do not need to upload your HTML file on a website or on the internet to view it. As long as your computer can access it, you can open it. And since your first HTML page will be in your computer, you can open it with your browser. After all, a web site can be viewed as a folder on the internet that contains HTML files that you can open.

When saving the file, make sure that it is being saved as plain text and not rich or formatted text. By default, programs such as Microsoft Word or WordPad save text files as formatted. If you saved the file as formatted, your browser might display the HTML code you have written incorrectly.

To open that file, you can try one of the three common ways. The first method is to double click or open the file normally. If you were able to save the file with the correct file extension, your computer will automatically open a browser to access the file.

The second method is to use the context menu (if you are using Windows). Right click on the file, and hover on the open with option. The menu will expand, and the list of programs that can open an HTML file will be displayed to you. Click on the browser that you want to use to open the file.

The third method is to open your browser. After that, type the local file address of your file. If you are using Windows 7 and you saved the file on the HTML folder in your desktop, then you can just type in C:\Users\User\Desktop\HTML\firstexample.html. The folder User may change depending on the account name you are using on your computer to login.

Once you have opened the file, it will show you the text you have written on it. Congratulations, you have already created a web page. You can just type paragraphs of text in the file, and it will be displayed by your browsers without problem. It is not the fanciest method, but it is the start of your journey to learn HTML.

You might be wondering, is it that easy? To be honest, yes. Were you expecting complex codes? Well, that will be tackled on the next chapter. And just to give you a heads up, it will not be complex.

This chapter has just given you an idea what is an HTML file and how you create, edit, and open one in your computer. The next chapter will discuss about tags, attributes, and elements.

Chapter 2: Elements, Properties, Tags, and Attributes

Of course, you might be already thinking: "Web pages do not contain text only, right?" Yes, you are right. In this part of the book, you will have a basic idea about how HTML code works, and how you can place some links on your page.

A web page is composed of elements. A picture on a website's gallery is an element. A paragraph on a website's article is also an element. A hyperlink that directs to another page is an element, too. But how can you do that with text alone? If you can create a web page by just using a text editor, how can you insert images on it?

Using Tags

Well, you can do that by using tags and attributes. By placing tags on the start and end of a text, you will be able to indicate what element it is. It might sound confusing, so below is an example for you to visualize and understand it better and faster:

<p>This is a paragraph that is enclosed on a paragraph tag. This is another sentence. And another sentence.</p>
In the example, the paragraph is enclosed with <p> and </p>. Those two are called HTML tags. If you enclose a block of text inside those two, the browser will understand that the block of text is a paragraph element.

Before you go in further about other HTML tags, take note that there is syntax to follow when enclosing text inside HTML tags. First, an HTML tag has two parts. The first part is the opening or starting tag. And the second part is the closing or ending tag.

The opening tag is enclosed on angled brackets or chevrons (the ones that you use to denote inequality – less and greater than signs). The closing tag, on the other hand, is also enclosed on angled brackets, but it includes a forward slash before the tag itself. The forward slash denotes that the tag is an ending tag.

Those two tags must come in pairs when you use them. However, there are HTML tags that do not require them. And they are called null or void tags. This will be discussed in another lesson. For now, stick on learning the usual HTML tags which require both opening and closing tags.

Attributes

When it comes to inserting images and links in your HTML file, you will need to use attributes. Elements have properties. The properties of each element may vary. For example, paragraph elements do not have the HREF property that anchor elements have (the HREF property and anchor element will be discussed shortly).

To change or edit those properties, you need to assign values using attributes tags. Remember, to indicate an element, use tags; to change values of the properties of elements, use attributes. However, the meanings and relations of those terms might change once you get past HTML and start learning doing CSS and JavaScript. Nevertheless, hold on to that basic idea first until you get further in web development.

Anyway, you will not actually use attributes, but you will need to indicate or assign values on them. Below is an example on how to insert a link on your web page that you will require you to assign a value on an attribute:

<a href="www.google.com" >Google</a>
If ever you copied that, pasted or written it on your HTML file, and open your file on a browser, you will see this:

Google

In the example above, the anchor or <a> HTML tag is used. Use the anchor tag when you want to embed a hyperlink or link in your page. Any text between the opening and closing tags of the anchor tag will become the text that will appear as the hyperlink. In the example, it is the word Google that is place between the tags and has appeared on the browser as the link.

You might have noticed the href="www.google.com" part. That part of the line determines on what page your link will direct to when you click it. That part is an example of attribute value assignment. HREF or hypertext reference is an attribute of the anchor tag.

By default, the anchor tag's value is "" or blank. In case that you do not assign any value to that attribute when you use the anchor tag, the anchor element will not become a hyperlink. Try copying and saving this line on your HTML file.

<a>Google</a>
When you open or refresh your HTML file, it will only show the word Google. It will not be underlined or will have a font color of blue. It will be just a regular text. If you hover on it, your mouse pointer will not change into the hand icon; if you click it, your browser will not do anything because the HREF value is blank.

By the way, when you assign a value on an element's or tag's attribute, you must follow proper syntax. The attribute value assignment must be inside the opening tag's chevrons and must be after the text inside the tag.

The attribute assignment must be separated from the tag with a space or spaces. The attribute's name must be type first. It must be followed by an equals sign. Then the value you want to assign to the attribute must follow the equals sign, and must be enclosed with double quotes or single quotes.

Take note, even if the number of spaces between the opening tag and the attribute assignment does not matter much, it is best that you only use one spaces for the sake of readability.

Also, you can place a space between the attribute name and the equals sign or a space between the equals sign and the value that you want to assign to the attribute. However, it is best to adhere to standard practice by not placing a space between them.

When it comes to the value that you want to assign, you can either enclosed them in double or single quotes, but you should never enclose them on a single quote and a double quote or vice versa. If you start with a single quote, end with a single quote, too. Using different quotes will bring problems to your code that will affect the way your browser will display your HTML file.

Nesting HTML Tags

What if you want to insert a link inside your paragraph? How can you do that? Well, in HTML, you can place or nest tags inside tags. Below is an example:

<p>This is a paragraph. If you want to go to Google, click this <a href="www.google.com" >link</a>.</p>

If you save that on your HTML file and open your file in your browser, it will appear like this:

This is a paragraph. If you want to go to Google, click this link.

When coding HTML, you will be nesting a lot of elements. Always remember that when nesting tags, never forget the location of the start and closing tags. Make sure that you always close the tags you insert inside a tag before closing the tag you are placing a tag inside on. If you get them mixed up, problems in your page's display will occur. Those tips might sound confusing, so below is an example of a mixed up tag:

<p>This is a paragraph. If you want to go to Google, click this <a href="www.google.com" >link</p>. And this is an example of tags getting mixed up and closed improperly.</a>

In the example, the closing tag for the paragraph tag came first before the closing tag of the anchor tag. If you copied, saved, and opened that, this is what you will get:

This is a paragraph. If you want to go to Google, click this link

. And this is an example of tag that was mixed up and closed improperly.

Since paragraphs are block elements (elements that will be always displayed on the next line and any element after them will be displayed on the next line), the last sentence was shifted to the next line. That is because the code has terminated the paragraph tag immediately.

Also, the anchor tag was closed on the end of the paragraph. Because of that, the word link up to the last word of the last sentence became a hyperlink. You should prevent that kind of mistakes, especially if you are going to code a huge HTML file and are using other complex tags that require a lot of nesting such as table tags. In addition, always be wary of the number of starting and ending tags you use. Missing tags or excess tags can also ruin your web page and fixing and looking for them is a pain.

This chapter has taught you the basic ideas about elements, properties, tags, and attributes. In coding HTML, you will be mostly fiddling around with them. In the next chapter, you will learn how to code a proper HTML document.

Chapter 3: The Standard Structure of HTML

As of now, all you can do are single lines on your HTML file. Though, you might have already tried making a page full of paragraphs and links – thanks to your new found knowledge about HTML tags and attributes. And you might be already hungry to learn more tags that you can use and attributes that you can assign values with.

However, before you tackle those tags and attributes, you should learn about the basic structure of an HTML document. The HTML file you have created is not following the standards of HTML. Even though it does work on your browser, it is not proper to just place random HTML tags on your web page on random places.

In this chapter, you will learn about the html, head, and body tags. And below is the standard structure of an HTML page where those three tags are used:

```
<!DOCTYPE html>
<html>
<head></head>
<body></body>
</html>
```

The Body and the Head

You can split an HTML document in two. The first part is composed of the things that the browser displays on your screen. And the second part is composed of the things that you will not see but is important to your document.

Call the first part as your HTML page's body. And call the second part as your HTML page's head. Every web page that you can see on the net are composed of these two parts. The tags that you have learned in the previous chapter are part of your HTML's body.

As you can see on the example, the head and body tag are nested inside the html tag. The head goes in first, while the body is the last one to appear. The order of the two is essential to your web page.

When coding in HTML, you should always place or nest all the tags or elements that your visitors will see on your HTML's body tag. On the other hand, any script or JavaScript code and styling line or CSS line that your visitors will not see must go into the head tag.

Scripts and styling lines must be read first by your browser. Even before the browser displays all the elements in your body tag, it must be already stylized and the scripts should be ready. And that is why the head tag goes first before the body.

If you place the styling lines on the end of the page, the browser may behave differently. For example, if the styling lines are placed at the end, the browser will display the elements on the screen first, and then once it reads the styling lines, the appearance of the page will change. On the other hand, if a button on your page gets clicked before the scripts for it was loaded because the scripts are placed on the end of the document, the browser will return an error.

Browsers and Checking the Source Code

Fortunately, if you forget to place the html, head, and body tags, modern browsers will automatically generate them for you. For example, try opening the HTML file that you created without the three tags with Google Chrome.

Once you open your file, press the F12 key to activate the developer console. As you can see, the html, head, and body tags were already generated for you in order to display your HTML file properly.

By the way, checking source codes is an important method that you should always use if you want to learn or imitate a website's HTML code. You can easily do it by using the developer console on Chrome or by using the context menu on other browsers and clicking on the View Page Source or View Source option.

Document Type Declaration

HTML has undergone multiple versions. As of now, the latest version is HTML5. With each version, some tags are introduced while some are deprecated. And some versions come with specifications that make them behave differently from each other. Because of that, HTML documents must include a document type declaration to make sure that your markup will be displayed just the way you wanted them to appear on your visitors' screens.

However, you do not need to worry about this a lot since it will certainly stick with HTML5, which will not be discussed in full in this book. In HTML5, document type declaration is useless, but is required. To satisfy this, all you need to do is place this on the beginning of your HTML files:

<!DOCTYPE html>
With all of those laid out, you can now create proper HTML documents. In the following chapters, the book will focus on providing you the tags that you will use the most while web developing.

Chapter 4: More HTML Tags

Now, it is time to make your HTML file to appear like a typical web page on the internet. And you can do that by learning the tags and attributes that are used in websites you stumble upon while you surf the web.

The Title Tag

First of all, you should give your web page a title. You can do that by using the <title> tag. The title of the page can be seen on the title bar and tab on your browser. If you bookmark your page, it will become the name of the bookmark. Also, it will appear on your taskbar if the page is active.

When using the title tag, place it inside the head tag. Below is an example:

```
<head>
        <title>This Is My New Web Page</title>
</head>
```

The Header Tags

If you want to organize the hierarchy of your titles and text on your web page's article, then you can take advantage of the header tags. If you place a line of text inside header tags, its formatting will change. Its font size will become bigger and its font weight (thickness) will become heavier. For example:

```
<h1> This Is the Title of This Article</h1>
<p>This is the introductory paragraph. This is another sentence. And this is the last sentence.</p>
```

If you try this example, this is what you will get:

This Is the Title of This Article

This is the introductory paragraph. This is another sentence. And this is the last sentence.

There are six levels of heading tags and they are: <h1>,<h2>,<h3>,<h4>,<h5>, and <h6>. Each level has different formatting. And as the level gets higher, the lesser formatting will be applied.

The Image Tag

First, start with pictures. You can insert pictures in your web page by using the <img> tag. By the way, the <img> tag is one of HTML tags that do not need closing tags, which are called null or empty tags. And for you to see how it works, check the example below:

<img src="http://upload.wikimedia.org/wikipedia/commons/thumb/8/80/Wikipedia-logo-v2.svg/150px-Wikipedia-logo-v2.svg.png" >

If you try that code and opened your HTML file, the Wikipedia logo will appear. As you can see, the <img> tag did not need a closing tag to work. As long as you place a valid value on its src (source) attribute, then an image will appear on your page. In case an image file is not present on the URL you placed on the source attribute, then a broken image picture will appear instead.

Image Format Tips

By the way, the <img> tag can display pictures with the following file types: PNG, JPEG or JPG, and GIF. Each image type has characteristics that you can take advantage of. If you are going to post photographs, it is best to convert them to JPG file format. The JPG offers decent file compression that can reduce the size of your photographs without losing too much quality.

If you need lossless quality or if you want to display a photo or image as is, then you should use PNG. The biggest drawback on PNG is that old browsers cannot read PNG images. But that is almost a thing of a past since only handful people use old versions of browsers.

On the other hand, if you want animated images on your site, then use GIFs. However, take note that the quality of GIF is not that high. The number of colors it can display is few unlike PNG and JPG. But because of that, its size is comparatively smaller than the two formats, which is why some web developers convert their sites' logos as GIF to conserve space and reduce loading time.

The Ordered and Unordered List

Surely, you will place lists on your web pages sooner or later. In HTML, you can create two types of lists: ordered and unordered. Ordered lists generate alphanumeric characters to denote sequence on your list while unordered lists generate symbols that only change depending on the list level.

To create ordered lists, use the <ol> and <li> tag. The <ol> tag defines that the list will be an ordered one, and the <li> or list item tag defines that its content is considered a list item on the list. Below is an example:

```
<h1>Animals</h1>
<ol>
      <li>dog</li>
      <li>cat</li>
      <li>mouse</li>
</ol>
```
This will be the result of that example:

Animals

1. dog

2. cat

3. mouse

On the other hand, if you want an unordered list, you will need to use the <ul> tag. Like the <ol> tag, you will still need to use the <li> tag to denote the list items. Below is an example:

```
<h1>Verbs</h1>
<ul>
     <li>walk</li>
     <li>jog</li>
     <li>run</li>
</ul>
```

This will be the result of that example:

Verbs

- walk

- jog

- run

Instead of numbers, the list used bullets instead. If ever you use the <li> tag without <ol> or <ul>, browsers will usually create them as unordered lists.

Nesting Lists

You can nest lists in HTML to display child lists. If you do that, the browser will accommodate it and apply the necessary tabs for the child list items. If you nest unordered lists, the bullets will be changed to fit the child list items. Below is an example:

```
<h1>Daily Schedule</h1>
<ul>
     <li>Morning</li>

     <ul>
          <li>Jog</li>
          <li>Shower</li>
          <li>Breakfast</li>
     </ul>
     <li>Afternoon</li>
     <ul>
          <li>Lunch</li>
          <li>Watch TV</li>
```

```
    </ul>
    <li>Evening</li>
    <ul>
        <li>Dinner</li>
        <li>Sleep</li>
    </ul>
</ul>
```

This will be the result of that example:

Daily Schedule

- Morning
  - Jog
  - Shower
  - Breakfast
- Afternoon
  - Lunch
  - Watch TV
- Evening
  - Dinner
  - Sleep

And with that, you should be ready to create a decent website of your own. But for now, practice using those tags. And experiment with them.

Conclusion

Thank you again for purchasing this book!

I hope this book was able to help you to become knowledgeable when it comes to HTML development. With the fundamentals you have learned, you can easily explore the vast and enjoyable world of web development. And that is no exaggeration.

The next step is to learn more tags and check out websites' sources. Also, look for HTML development tips. Then learn more about HTML5 and schema markup. Those things will help you create richer web sites that are semantically optimized.

On the other hand, if you want to make your website to look cool, then you can jump straight to leaning CSS or Cascading Style Sheets. Cascading Style Sheets will allow you to define the appearance of all or each element in your web page. You can change font size, weight, color, and family of all the text on your page in a whim. You can even create simple animations that can make your website look modern and fancy.

If you want your website to be interactive, then you can start learning client side scripting with JavaScript or Jscript too. Scripts will provide your web pages with functions that can make it more alive. An example of a script function is when you press a button on your page, a small window will popup.

Once you master all of that, then it will be the best time for you to start learning server side scripting such as PHP or ASP. With server side scripting, you can almost perform everything on websites. You can take information from forms and save them to your database. Heck, you can even create dynamic web pages. Or even add chat functions on your website.

Finally, if you enjoyed this book, please take the time to share your thoughts and post a review on Amazon. We do our best to reach out to readers and provide the best value we can. Your positive review will help us achieve that. It'd be greatly appreciated!

Thank you and good luck!

Check Out My Other Books

Below you'll find some of my other popular books that are popular on Amazon and Kindle as well. Simply click on the links below to check them out. Alternatively, you can visit my author page on Amazon to see other work done by me.

C Programming Success in a Day

Android Programming in a Day

C Programming Professional Made Easy

C ++ Programming Success in a Day

Python Programming in a Day

PHP Programming Professional Made Easy

JavaScript Programming Made Easy

CSS Programming Professional Made Easy

Windows 8 Tips for Beginners

Programming Box Set #80: Android Programming in a Day & HTML Professional Programming Made Easy

If the links do not work, for whatever reason, you can simply search for these titles on the Amazon website to find them.

www.ingramcontent.com/pod-product-compliance
Lightning Source LLC
Chambersburg PA
CBHW060928050326
40689CB00013B/3012